THE SPREAD OF DESERTS

Ewan McLeish

Conserving Our World

Acid Rain
Conserving Rainforests
Waste and Recycling
Conserving the Atmosphere
Protecting Wildlife
The Spread of Deserts
Farming and the Environment
Protecting the Oceans

Cover: The Taghit oasis, Algeria

Series editor: Sue Hadden
Series designer: Ross George
Editor: Alison Cooper

First published in 1989 by
Wayland (Publishers) Ltd
61 Western Road, Hove,
East Sussex BN3 1JD, England

British Library Cataloguing in Publication Data
McLeish, Ewan
　The spread of deserts. – (Conserving our world)
　1. Desertification
　I. Title　II. Series
　333.73

ISBN 1 85210 699 9

Typeset by Kalligraphics Ltd, Horley, Surrey
Printed in Italy by G. Canale & C. S.p.A., Turin

Contents

A lifeless desert?

The sun beats down on the baked surface of the Arizona desert in the USA. It has not rained for over a year. There is no sign of life.

A few small, white clouds appear in the vast blue sky. They grow rapidly. A shaft of lightning splits the gathering darkness, and the rain comes. Huge raindrops explode on the parched ground.

In ten minutes it is over; the sun shines as brightly as ever. It will not rain again for another year, perhaps longer. But something is happening on the seemingly lifeless desert floor. A clump of dead and withered plants begins to move. The dry and brittle seed heads, swollen by the rain, snap open, hurling out a shower of seeds on to the moist ground.

Then the ground itself begins to stir. The surface of the earth cracks and hundreds of creatures that have been lying dormant for many months clamber out into the sunlight. They are spadefoot toads. The males quickly find the shallow pools that have formed after the rains; soon they are joined by females and, within a day, eggs are laid and fertilized. A day later young tadpoles are feeding hungrily on the microscopic plants now growing in the warm waters.

But now something even stranger happens. Some of the tadpoles begin to develop huge heads and mouths. They turn on their smaller brothers and sisters and eat them. In this way, if no further rain comes, a few large and aggressive individuals will survive in the centre of the rapidly shrinking pools; if they are lucky they will have time to develop into young toads before the pools dry up completely. They will form the next generation of spadefoots. Soon, they begin to burrow into the mud, sealing themselves in their underground burrows until the rains return.

Above The desert comes to life, as wild flowers bloom after the rain. Rain may not return to this area for another year.

Left A thunderstorm approaches in the Arizona desert, USA.

Above When the rains return, the adult spadefoot toads emerge from the sand.

Left Spadefoot tadpoles jostle for space in the rapidly shrinking pools. Only the largest and most aggressive will survive to become toads.

A dying land

Talah is 13 years old. Until recently she lived with her three brothers and two sisters in a small village in southern Niger, a central African country to the south of the great Sahara Desert. Life had always been hard, and harder than ever since the family had been forced on to poorer land by the big cotton-growing company. But now the rains had failed two years in a row and the millet crop, on which the family depended, had withered and died.

The drought was only part of the problem. Several wells had been dug nearby to bring a more reliable water supply to the village. But the project had been a disaster almost from the start. The water had attracted the goatherds of travelling stockmen to the area. The goats had eaten everything in sight and their trampling had destroyed the struggling grass. Without the cover of vegetation, the thin soil began to blow

The goats kill the smaller trees; the larger trees will be cut down for extra fodder or firewood.

away. Soon nothing would grow. Even the few trees that used to grow around the village had gone, perhaps cut down for desperately-needed firewood by the villagers, or taken at night in trucks by illegal traders, to be sold as charcoal in the overcrowded city 40 km away.

When their last supplies of food ran out, Talah and her family were forced to leave the village. They had heard of a camp 60 km to the south where food was being brought in by lorry. They did not want to abandon their home but already Talah's younger brother was ill from lack of food.

They walked for three days across the barren land; three days without food and hardly any water. On the fourth day Talah's brother died. On the fifth day they reached the relief camp. They erected a makeshift tent and received a kilo of rice, and water from the single well.

They are there now. Talah dreams about her village and of returning there one day. But it is not a village any more, a place where crops were grown and sheep reared, and life went on from day to day and from generation to generation. There is no life there now; it has become a desert.

The spread of deserts

These two stories have something in common – they are both true and they are both about deserts. But there the similarity ends. The first story is about a natural desert, an area that has existed for thousands, perhaps millions of years. Over that time animals and plants, and even people, have learned how to live with its soaring temperatures and meagre rainfall.

The second story is about a desert that has been created in months or even days. It is not natural because it has been created by people.

Right Women and children queue for water at the camp in Niger, as abandoned villages (below) become part of the desert.

Nothing has learned to live in it; it may never return to what it was before. And it is spreading.

This book is mainly about the second type of desert: why it happens, and why, in different ways, we are all responsible. It is a serious story, but not a hopeless one. This book is also about how the spread of deserts can be stopped. You may think that this is someone else's problem: this book is also about why you could be wrong.

The living desert

This chapter looks more closely at deserts: how they form and what lives in them. It is also the key to understanding how deserts spread.

What are deserts?

Deserts occur naturally all over the world. Most are found near the Tropic of Cancer and the Tropic of Capricorn, where the sun is strong and the winds bring virtually no rain.

But deserts are spreading and much of this is not natural. It is caused by the way that humans treat the land on which they depend.

In films, deserts are always shown as endless seas of shifting sand, with the hero staggering from dune to dune before finally collapsing at a handy oasis. Some deserts are like this, but most are made up of bare rock, boulders and gravel.

Even so, deserts like the Sahara contain vast areas of sand which are constantly on the move, threatening to engulf villages and oases as the wind moves them relentlessly onwards.

Deserts are huge. They make up more than 12 per cent of the earth's land surface. The Sahara stretches from the Red Sea 5,000 km west to the Atlantic Ocean. Some of its sand dunes may be 300 m high. The Australian desert covers nearly 80 per cent of the country's land surface.

Above *This building was once a telegraph station in Eucla, Western Australia. Soon it will be buried by the drifting sand.*

Right *Most of the world's deserts occur around the tropics.*

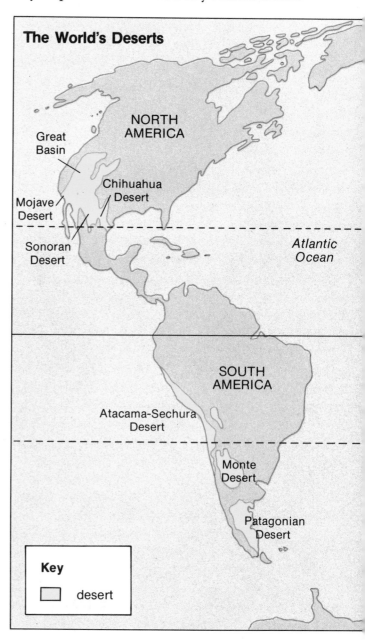

The World's Deserts

NORTH AMERICA

Great Basin

Chihuahua Desert

Mojave Desert

Sonoran Desert

Atlantic Ocean

SOUTH AMERICA

Atacama-Sechura Desert

Monte Desert

Patagonian Desert

Key

☐ desert

Temperatures in deserts usually reach over 25°C in the shade every day, and often reach the low forties (the record is 58°C in Libya). But at night, deserts become very cold as the heat escapes into the cloudless sky; it may even freeze. Some deserts in central Asia are called cold deserts, with hot summers but cold winters.

Right *In deserts, what little rain there is falls over a very short period.*

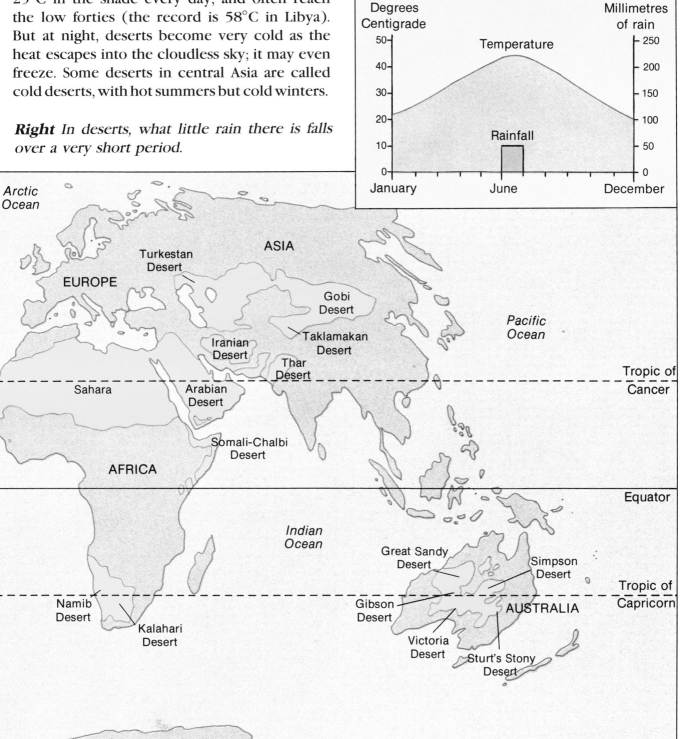

Nevada, Great Basin, USA

Degrees Centigrade

Millimetres of rain

Temperature

Rainfall

January June December

Arctic Ocean

ASIA

Turkestan Desert

EUROPE

Gobi Desert

Iranian Desert

Taklamakan Desert

Thar Desert

Sahara

Arabian Desert

Pacific Ocean

Tropic of Cancer

Somali-Chalbi Desert

AFRICA

Equator

Indian Ocean

Great Sandy Desert

Simpson Desert

Namib Desert

Gibson Desert

AUSTRALIA

Tropic of Capricorn

Kalahari Desert

Victoria Desert

Sturt's Stony Desert

ANTARCTICA

Dry Valleys

rising hot air can lead to violent thunderstorms

dry winds and hot sun produce deserts

winds lose moisture in rainfall as they pass over mountains

North East Trade Winds

desert

South East Trade Winds

moisture bearing winds

Deserts are the driest places in the world. Rain may not fall for several years; in some parts of the Atacama Desert in South America it is reputed not to have rained for 400 years! Usually there is less than 20 cm of rain per year. Often it falls over a very short period during violent thunderstorms.

Have deserts always been deserts?

Ancient rock paintings have been found in desert areas all over the African continent. Some, found in caves in the Sahara, are over 5,000 years old. The rock paintings show cattle, wild animals and hunters. This suggests that even these great deserts were once fertile enough for people to live not only by hunting and gathering but by raising domestic animals. Changes in the climate have made the deserts what they are today.

These rock engravings of wild animals were found at Twyfelfontein in Namibia.

Deserts occur where the wind has passed over thousands of miles of land or over mountain ranges, losing all its moisture as it does so.

Life in the deserts

Many things live in deserts. These include animals, plants and people. Often they have special ways of behaving, or special features (adaptations) which enable them to survive.

Look again at the first story in the Introduction. What do you think are the main difficulties that living things have to face in order to survive in a desert? Write them down. Now write a list of the ways in which the animals are adapted to cope with some of these difficulties.

Some more desert animals and plants are illustrated below. Some of the ways in which they are adapted to survive in deserts are shown.

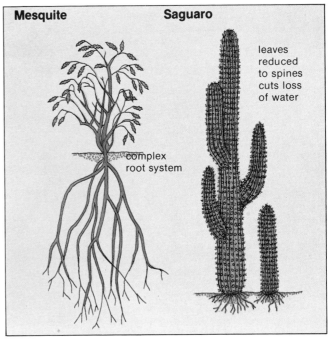

When the sun becomes too hot the Kalahari ground squirrel will raise its tail like a parasol.

*Desert plants (**above**) are able to extract every drop of moisture from the soil and they are adapted to reduce the loss of water by evaporation. The hard outer case of the scorpion (**left**) also helps to reduce water loss. Namibian sand grouse (**below**) soak their breast feathers in water and carry it back to their young.*

11

Night life

Even with their excellent adaptations, few animals could survive the savage midday temperatures. So they tend to stay under cover during much of the day, sheltering under boulders, or in burrows. Here it is not only cooler, but also damper, for the animals' own breath raises the humidity of the surrounding air. This means they lose less moisture from their bodies by evaporation.

As the sun begins to set, the desert stirs. In the Sahara, mouse-like gerbils and long-legged,

The huge ears of the fennec fox act as cooling devices, enabling body heat to escape from their large surface area. They also pick up even the faintest scrabbling of a jerboa. The fennec gets all its liquid requirements from its prey.

hopping jerboas appear from their burrows, searching for seeds or pieces of dead vegetation. The hunters are also out: geckos scurry between rocks, looking for beetles, while fennec foxes, huge ears alert, trail the ground for scents that will lead them to an unsuspecting gerbil.

The story is the same in deserts all over the world; only the animals change. In the North American desert the kit fox replaces the fennec; in the Australian outback, the rat kangaroo takes the place of the jerboa.

But the nights become very cold. Those animals that rely on the warmth of their surroundings to maintain their body temperature ('cold-blooded' animals such as lizards, snakes, insects and scorpions), begin to slow down as the temperature falls. Soon they have to stop hunting for food and retire to their crevices until the following evening. Even the warm-blooded mammals – the foxes, jerboas, and mice – find it too cold for their liking and return to their dens and burrows well before dawn.

The day shift

As the sun rises, a new set of animals appear. In the dry lands of the American West, the Gila (pronounced 'heela') monster begins its daily patrol. As the sun warms its stumpy body, it snaps up insects, birds' eggs and even nestlings. In Australia, the moloch lizard has to find and consume 7,000 ants for breakfast, its only meal of the day. Before long the rapidly increasing heat will force it, and the other members of the day shift, back into shelter.

The bright coloration of the Gila monster is a warning to predators. It is one of only two poisonous lizards that exist.

The survival game

An Aboriginal bushman walks through the red desert of central Australia. He is looking for water. His keen eyes miss nothing: the tracks of small creatures, the shape of rocks, the few straggling plants. He stops at a seemingly dead stem from which hang a couple of tattered leaves. He starts to dig with a stick; the stem begins to thicken; half a metre below the surface it becomes a root the size of a football. The root is pulled up, grated with a knife and squeezed between his hands. A trickle of liquid appears. The bushman drinks. There is no other water within a hundred kilometres.

The ability to survive in extreme desert conditions is rare; perhaps only the bushmen of Australia and Africa can obtain all their needs from these inhospitable parts of the world. They read their surroundings like a book, looking for signs that mean food or water, healing plants or a safe resting place.

Right The Australian bushmen use every part of the environment; this natural 'sound shell' magnifies the smallest sound.

Below The Australian outback; imagine having to obtain everything you need to survive from this inhospitable land.

The bushmen carry with them a store of knowledge and understanding about their environment that is so complex that it would baffle most biologists. And all of it is passed on from generation to generation in songs and stories; not a word is written down. Perhaps it could be said that, because they understand their environment, they respect it; and because they respect it, they are able to live in harmony with it.

The nomads

The bushmen are not the only human inhabitants of the desert, however. Many people live at its borders or travel through it. The Tuareg, who came originally from the northern side of the Sahara, regularly lead convoys (caravans) across it, carrying bronze or gold, dates and silk, to exchange for salt in the ancient trading cities on the River Niger.

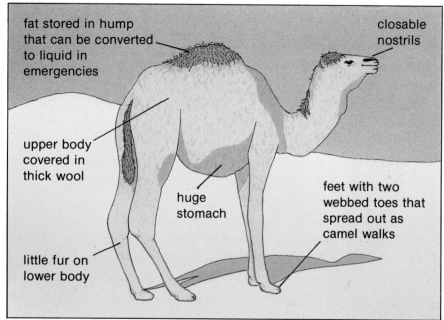

fat stored in hump that can be converted to liquid in emergencies

closable nostrils

upper body covered in thick wool

huge stomach

feet with two webbed toes that spread out as camel walks

little fur on lower body

Above *A caravan of Tuareg nomads crosses the edge of the Sahara; how are the nomads equipped to withstand the sun?*

Left *How do you think the adaptations shown in this diagram help the camel to survive in the desert?*

Nomads could not cross the desert without the aid of an extraordinary animal – the camel. The camel has many special adaptations which help it to survive in the desert. The camel, however, depends also on its human companions. It could not survive a crossing of the Sahara without the Tuareg to haul water from the wells at the oases that occur occasionally in the desert. Here water-bearing rocks come closer to the surface and form natural pools or sites for wells. Here too the desert is suddenly transformed into a fertile garden of date palms, tended cereal crops and even peaches. Perhaps this was what the desert was like thousands of years ago, before the climate changed and the rains went away. But even here, in the background, the sand dunes loom, ready to engulf the oasis in one great sandstorm. For the desert is always on the move.

At this oasis in Tunisia the barren desert is transformed into fertile land. But the desert's shifting sand is an ever-present threat.

The desert spreads

Have you ever been out for a walk after a heavy rainstorm? Often the roads are covered with a thin layer of mud or gravel washed out from the surrounding area.

Have you noticed what happens when people take a short cut across the grass? Soon a track of bare mud forms. Even animals like deer, sheep and rabbits rapidly wear away paths across fields. Like humans, they tend to stick to the quickest route!

Have you ever heard the wind whistling down the street and felt the dust stinging as it flies up in your face?

Most of the time we hardly notice these things. But imagine them magnified ten, a hundred, a million times. Then we can begin to understand how deserts spread.

Left Whatever planners want, people take the shortest route ... and so do animals. This path (right) has been worn by foxes and badgers.

Deserts in Britain?

Much of East Anglia is low-lying, fertile and flat. In recent years many of the hedges and trees surrounding fields were removed to make the fields bigger. This allowed combine harvesters to work more efficiently. But it also meant that there were no longer barriers to stop the wind and rain from lashing across the land, whipping up large quantities of soil and washing or blowing it into rivers and ditches. East Anglia is not a desert, but the process of erosion is the same as that which creates deserts elsewhere.

18

The Great Dustbowl.

After the First World War, falling cereal prices and the need to keep up payments on their new tractors forced farmers in the Great Plains of the American Midwest to plough up more and more land to increase wheat production. This land was often unsuitable for growing cereals and now farmers could no longer afford to leave fields to recover between crops (a practice known as lying fallow). As a result the quality of the soil worsened rapidly.

Then, in 1930 and 1931, there were two years of drought. Wheat was left in the ground because it was not worth harvesting. Cattle died and farmers could not meet their debts. Thousands were forced to migrate west to California.

In 1934, a gale raged across America: 350 million tonnes of dust that had once been the topsoil of Kansas, Montana and the Dakotas just blew away. The sun was eclipsed and cities like Washington and New York were plunged into darkness. The area became known as the Great Dustbowl. It had become a desert.

Making connections

You will notice that there are many similarities between these stories and the story about Talah and her family in Africa (*see* Introduction). They are about the effect that people have on their surroundings. You may also have noticed that neither of these stories is simple; each is a complicated chain of events in which every action has an effect on something else. Understanding these links is important if we are to understand how deserts spread and how it may be possible to stop them.

In the 1930s, a combination of drought and economic depression brought ruin to thousands of farmers in the American Midwest. Many left their homes, hoping to start a new life in California but instead endured terrible hardship. John Steinbeck tells their story in his powerful novel The Grapes of Wrath.

How deserts spread

If deserts are a natural part of our planet, what is the problem? The problem is that deserts are surrounded by vast areas of what is called arid and semi-arid land. Arid really means 'dry', although not as dry as deserts. Arid land has an annual rainfall of about 20-25 cm and semi-arid land 25-60 cm. Most of the rain falls at one time of year but, in some years, the rains fail to come and there is drought. Arid and semi-arid areas are usually covered with grassland or scrub – bushes and small trees. They are often very fertile and ideal for cultivation and for raising livestock. This is where the problem begins.

All areas undergo change; it is a natural part of life. A field, if it is left alone, will eventually become a forest; a pond will gradually become dry land as vegetation dies and builds up. Arid and semi-arid lands also change over a number

of years, depending on how they are used and on changes in the local climate. They may change from grassland to quite dense scrub and then revert to grassland.

These changes do no harm; they are part of a natural cycle. A change to grassland will help the rancher who wants more grass for his cattle; a change to scrub will provide fuel wood for the village. But this cycle can be interrupted. If the rancher brings in too many cattle, or the villagers

Above *People living in arid regions need firewood but when too many trees are cut down, the exposed soil becomes eroded and the desert spreads.*

Left *This semi-arid land in Israel is very fertile; but it is also very vulnerable and easily destroyed by over-cultivation.*

cut too much firewood, a different kind of change occurs. The vegetation is damaged and becomes thinner. The soil is exposed and is more easily washed away when the rains come, or blown away in the dry season. This process is called erosion.

Up to this point the damage may be reversed and the land will recover if the rancher reduces his herds or less wood is cut. If not, the fertile part of the soil, the topsoil, is lost and recovery may be impossible. The change is no longer a cycle but a one-way decline towards destruction. This is how desertification – the spread of deserts – begins.

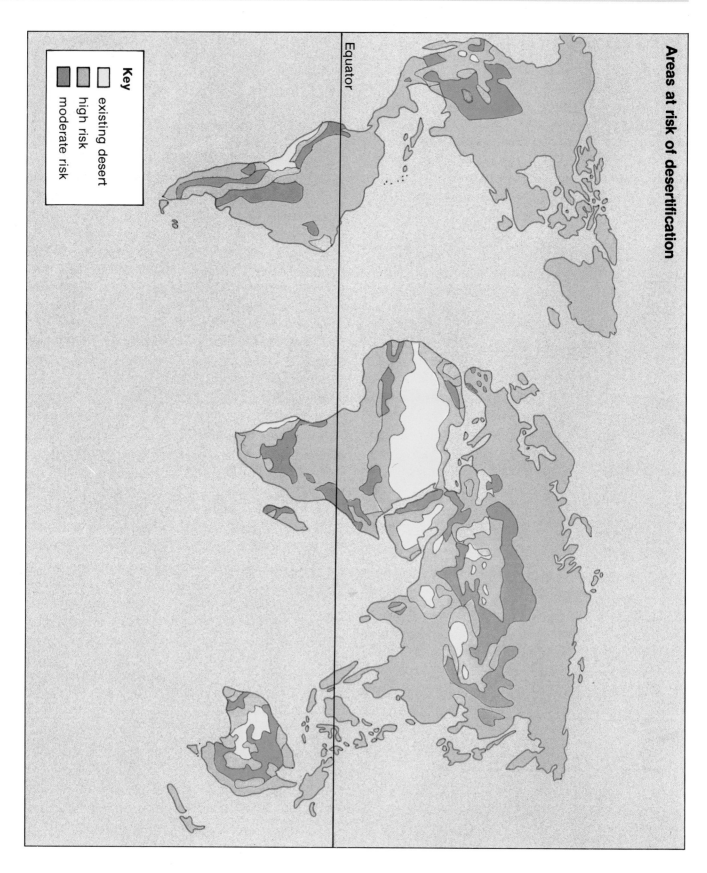

Equator

Key

existing desert

high risk

moderate risk

Above *Counting the cost: this is the human result of desertification.*

The areas affected

It is hard to imagine the scale on which the spread of deserts is taking place. For example:

● One third of the earth's land surface is arid or semi-arid, home to more than 600 million people. More than half this area is under direct threat of desertification.

● The spread of deserts is global, affecting two-thirds of the world's nations. It is not limited to the so-called developing countries, although they may be hardest hit by its effects. In the United States, Canada, and Mexico a larger area (10.5 million sq km) is estimated to be affected than on the entire African continent south of the Sahara (6.9 million sq km).

The effects on people

The spread of deserts affects people – usually poor people in rural areas with small incomes and little or no land. Perhaps it starts with the failure of the rains, or perhaps the soil has already begun to grow poorer as too much is asked of it by a growing population. Crops fail and sheep or cattle begin to die of starvation or disease. Surviving livestock are forced to search larger areas for their food, damaging the land; farmers are forced to move on to steep hillside land or areas previously considered too infertile for cultivation. Trees are cut down to provide fodder for the starving animals. The wind begins to blow away the dry soil and the desert spreads.

However, the hardship is only just beginning. Eventually the people must either move or starve. Many find their way to camps; others may reach cities or even other countries; some never arrive. Even in the cities there is no end to the suffering: no jobs, little food, poor shelter, overcrowding, unhygienic conditions, and disease. This is the human result of the spread of deserts.

Desert sand covers a village street in Chad.

Why deserts spread

If you ask people what causes deserts and the famines that result from them, most will probably answer 'drought'. It seems obvious. But look again at the story about Talah in the Introduction. This time write a list of some of the causes of the situation in which her family finds itself. How many are to do with drought? Now look at the causes more closely; how many are due to the actions of Talah's family and how many are outside their control?

You should by now be getting some idea of how complex the factors behind the spread of deserts really are. This chapter looks more closely at some of the causes of desertification, and how they combine to make an already difficult situation into an impossible one.

Women pounding millet in Mali, West Africa. Millet, a traditional crop, is adapted to grow in semi-arid conditions.

TOO MANY CROPS SPOIL THE SOIL

Although arid and semi-arid lands are fertile, they have a low humus content. This means they do not contain a large quantity of organic material (dead plant and animal matter). In the past, after four or five years of growing crops, the land would be left fallow or used as pasture for grazing for several years. During this time, the soil would be protected by a covering of vegetation, vital nutrients could build up, and the humus content would increase.

This was not the only way that farmers protected both themselves and their land. A number of different crops were sown to reduce the risks of a total crop failure; drought-resistant crops such as sorghum and millet were used; dung from the cattle of the nomadic herders helped regenerate the exhausted soil and cereals could be bartered (traded) for meat. Little cash ever changed hands.

Methods like these evolved over thousands of years to make the best use of what was available, just as the animals and plants in the second chapter evolved ways of surviving.

The human factor

In recent years human populations in many countries throughout the world have increased dramatically. More people need more food; more food means that more land is cultivated, or existing land is used more intensively (more food is obtained from the same amount of land). As a result, traditional methods of agriculture have been lost; fallow periods get shorter and disappear; areas that are drier and better suited to grazing come under cultivation. The fertility of the soil falls and therefore less, rather than more, food is produced.

A market in Morocco. Often little money changes hands, as animals are exchanged for grain or vegetables. It is important to understand that these animals are often the only form of wealth that the herdsmen have.

Cash crops

When you sit down to a meal which includes tea, coffee, chocolate, or bananas; when you put on a cotton shirt in the morning, or buy a packet of peanuts, then you are involved in the spread of deserts.

How? All countries need exports to pay for the goods they buy from other nations. One way is to grow crops that other countries want but cannot, or will not, grow themselves. They are called cash crops. Often a country may find it is exporting food while its own people go hungry. For example, during the famines in the Sahel in the 1970s, food exports such as groundnuts (peanuts), actually increased while people of the Sahel starved to death. A similar situation occurs in Mexico. Here 80 per cent of children in rural areas are undernourished, but livestock eat more grain than the entire population. Ironically the livestock is mainly exported and ends up as hamburgers in rich countries like the USA.

The best land is often used for cash crop plantations. Small farmers may be forced to work for the plantation owners, or else move on to poorer land. The cash crops themselves are often unsuited to the conditions, requiring constant treatment from expensive fertilizers and pesticides. Eventually the land again suffers from over-use and the build-up of chemicals. Meanwhile, the poorer land, having to support too many people, rapidly turns into desert.

Many cash crops have to be grown in artificial conditions. How well protected from the pesticide spray is the farmer?

It is easy to see that systems like this are unfair and unjust. But they are also very complicated. Often the countries involved are in debt to the richer nations in Europe and North America, and desperately need 'foreign exchange' to pay their bills. It is important to understand that the spread of deserts is not just a question of too many people or unfortunate weather. It is also a political question.

Irrigation schemes

Irrigation – bringing water to waterless or drought-hit areas by digging wells or building canals – is one way of growing more food in arid areas. Irrigation schemes provide water for 2.5 million sq km of farmland; this is 13 per cent of all land under cultivation in the world.

The advantages:

● Irrigation can lead to a six-fold increase in the yield of cereals and other crops.

● Irrigation can reduce the threat of crop failure during droughts, and stop desertification by slowing down the movement of farmers on to poorer land.

The disadvantages:

● Irrigation projects mean large profits for construction and other companies, usually in the richer countries. This may mean more debt and even unnecessary or unwanted projects in the arid countries.

● If not properly designed and managed, irrigation can turn land into desert.

If irrigated land is not properly drained, the soil becomes waterlogged. Then salts in the soil or in the irrigation water itself build up and the land becomes useless for growing crops. This process is called salinization. The land is abandoned, the natural vegetation dies and more desert is created.

Small irrigation projects like this in Northern Cameroon can greatly increase crop yields. But badly managed projects can create deserts.

Irrigation can create other problems too. If there are too many wells, the water table – the level at which water is present below the ground – may fall. Eventually the wells become dry and the land is abandoned. Where canals are dug, the slow-moving or stagnant water attracts disease-carrying mosquitoes or the snails that carry the blinding disease, bilharzia. Irrigation projects may also attract mobile herders. Then a new problem arises: overgrazing.

THE PRESSURE ON PASTURES

Traditionally, people keeping herds in arid lands have been nomadic, that is they moved with their herds of sheep, goats, cattle or even camels to where pasture could be found. They understood the land well, knowing where rain or the local geography had created good feeding for their livestock. They moved frequently, spreading their herds widely over the sparse vegetation. In this way, the pastures or rangelands were maintained.

As the human population increased, so did the size and number of their herds. In addition the nomads became poorer as their traditional trade in salt, bronze, gold and sometimes even arms, declined.

So now the only way in which the herders can save for the future is to increase the size of the herds. In good years the herds are allowed to increase rapidly. But with the first signs of drought, the herdsmen are reluctant to sell or kill animals since they are now their only form of wealth. It is not hard to predict what happens.

As the amount of land under cultivation spreads, much of the traditional grazing land at the margins of the deserts is ploughed up. Animals become concentrated into smaller areas and the old migration routes followed by the nomads are disturbed. The result is more overgrazing, and now the old co-operation between the herdsmen and the farmers breaks down too.

Nomads are a problem to a government: they are difficult to tax; they cross frontiers and perhaps carry arms; their constant movement makes education and health care difficult; they come into conflict with farmers and their herds are blamed for causing erosion. So what better solution than to get them to settle down? Think of some arguments for and against the settlement of nomadic people. How could their settlement contribute to the spread of deserts?

This soil erosion in Kenya is the result of overgrazing. Now the land is bare, the rain will rapidly wash it away, forming deep gullies as it does so.

It is easy to think that these problems are confined to the developing countries. But in the dry areas of countries like the USA, Canada and Australia, large ranches cause the same problems as nomadic herding.

Western-style ranches are springing up in Africa, to produce beef for export. But they are rarely successful and the ranch owners face many of the problems encountered by the growers of cash crops. Production is poor, there are problems of transport to markets, and land previously available to nomadic herders is closed off.

Rangelands or wastelands?

In the USA more than half of the privately owned rangelands are overgrazed, and soil erosion has halved the possible grass production.
A survey of a 64,000 sq km area in the Gascoyne Basin of north-west Western Australia showed that, after sixty years of heavy sheep grazing, 15 per cent of the area was so badly eroded that further grazing would damage it irreversibly.
Overgrazing by animals introduced by European settlers – cattle, horses and rabbits – is the main cause of desertification in central

A dried-up water hole in New South Wales, Australia. This desert has been caused by over-grazing.

Australia's arid zone. This has led to the extinction of a large number of native species of plants and animals. Many of those that remain are now also threatened.

THE DISAPPEARING FORESTS

Deforestation is becoming a familiar word. It means the cutting down of woods and forests without replacing them. Most people think of tropical rain forests in this connection, but the loss of open woodland in the arid lands is just as serious. It is one of the major causes of the spread of deserts.

About 90 per cent of people in the developing world depend on wood for building and as their main source of fuel – for cooking and for heating during the cold nights, for making bricks and many other uses. It is collected locally, mostly by women, usually as fallen branches or brushwood. But as populations increase and land is cleared for agriculture or cash-crop plantations, trees are cut down. Gradually, areas around villages become cleared of trees and, as one conservationist said," When trees go, deserts come."

The demand for charcoal and wood from the growing populations in the cities puts more pressure on the diminishing supply. Although most tree felling is illegal, there is a huge black market in wood in many countries, with well-organized syndicates bringing fuel wood by truck and camel into the cities.

Fuelwood

Women in the Upper Volta may have to walk for four to six hours, three times a week, to gather wood to cook the evening meal.
In urban areas, families spend as much as a quarter of their income on buying fuel wood or charcoal.

Wood piles on the River Niger. As wood becomes more scarce, its price rises and many people are unable to afford it.

In some countries trees hold back the monsoon rains and release them gradually. Deforestation in the Himalayas now results in regular flooding of several Indian states, such as West Bengal and Uttar Pradesh. The floods bring down millions of tonnes of soil and silt from the lower mountain slopes. The silt clogs up the rivers and reservoirs. In 1979 a dam above the industrial town of Morvi in Western Gujaret, India, became so full of silt that it was unable to hold back the flood waters streaming down from the Himalayas. The dam burst; a wall of water and mud buried the town: 15,000 people died.

The vicious circle

This chapter has looked at just some of the factors causing the spread of deserts. There are many others. Some climatologists think that the weather itself in arid areas is changing and that they are becoming drier. It may be that the spreading deserts alter the climate, since the vanishing vegetation no longer draws up water from the ground into the air, creating rain.

However three things are clear: firstly, droughts by themselves do not create deserts — they just make a bad situation worse; secondly, people do cause deserts but in very complicated ways and often for reasons outside their control. Finally, if people create deserts it should follow that they can also stop them.

Can deserts be turned back?

It is easy to think of people affected by the spread of deserts as helpless victims of events beyond their control. This would be wrong. For a start, people show immense courage and resourcefulness in situations which we find almost impossible to imagine. Most of the time they cope reasonably well. They are also equally capable of making decisions about their future and the future of their land. This is why the spread of deserts can be stopped.

Why we fail

In 1977, following severe droughts and appalling loss of life in the Sahel, the United Nations held an international conference on the spread of deserts. The conference made many proposals to halt, and turn back, the advancing deserts.

Now, over ten years later, few of those plans have been put into action; desertification still remains the biggest single threat to a quarter of the world's population. Why? First we need to look at some basic questions.

Does foreign aid help?

Disasters such as those in Ethiopia and the Sudan in 1984 and 1985 resulted in enormous sums of money being raised, both by voluntary organizations such as Oxfam and Save the Children, and by national governments.

Unfortunately, all too often, the aid misses the mark. This is especially true of aid given by other governments. Often it is linked to construction projects, such as road building, because they are reasonably easy to carry out. Other aid goes to

The problem of providing adequate water supplies is of major concern to both national governments and relief agencies. In rural areas the problem is often made worse, as domestic animals crowd around the water tanks that are provided. Eventually, this can cause severe erosion.

Above Emergency aid for the Sudan is unloaded at Khartoum. Poor communications, bad weather and sometimes civil war can make it difficult to distribute aid to those in most need.

irrigation projects. Although some projects are successful, others create deserts by concentrating domestic animals around water holes and by causing salinization. Huge quantities of aid also go into the towns and cities, where populations are rising rapidly and systems like water supplies and drainage are breaking down.

It has been estimated that only 24 per cent of all aid going to the Sahel is spent on the improvement of agriculture and forestry. Much of this is still spent on the development of cash crops for export.

Why does food aid cause problems?

There is so much talk about food mountains in Europe and other countries that it seems obvious to send it to countries where it is needed. But although food aid saves lives in emergencies, the problems of delivery are enormous; much of it ends up on the 'black market' where it is resold at high prices by unscrupulous dealers, and most of it goes to the cities. Perhaps more importantly, cereals such as wheat and rice, brought in from other countries, push down the price of local produce such as millet and sorghum, and many local farmers go out of business or have to turn to the production of cash crops.

Food aid alone cannot stop the spread of deserts; often it adds to the problem.

Could the countries affected do something about the size of their populations?

Population is a factor in the spread of deserts but consider this: the USA has 6 per cent of the world's population and consumes 25 per cent of the world's resources. It also has a big desertification problem. Should it 'do something' to control the size of its population?

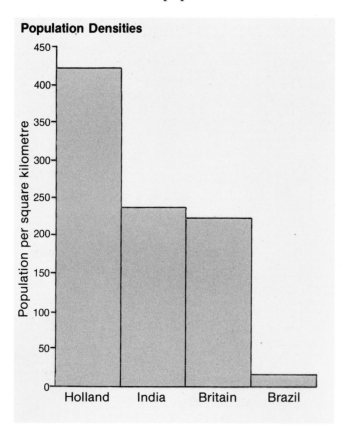

Population Densities

Above The poorest countries are not the ones with the highest population densities.

The hungry countries where deserts are spreading are not the ones which are the most densely populated, or which consume the most. But they are the countries where the poor are not given access to land to grow food – or money to buy it.

Why don't the governments of the countries concerned try to prevent desertification?

Many governments *do* try, but many of the causes are outside their control. Desertification crosses many national boundaries, so co-operation between countries is needed. Some of the countries have internal problems like civil war; many are poor and in debt to the richer nations.

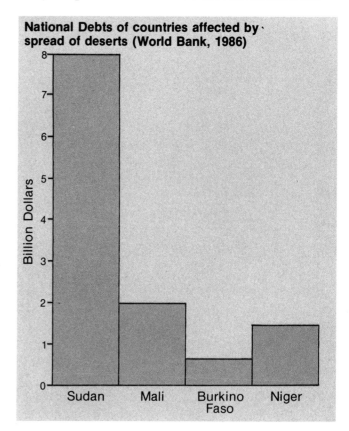

National Debts of countries affected by spread of deserts (World Bank, 1986)

Above As the table indicates, many developing countries suffer from serious economic problems. They often cannot afford to invest in long-term measures to prevent desertification.

A United Nations' expert's view:
'It takes an enormous time to change the thinking of people. Yet we need a complete change in thinking by everybody.'

How to succeed

Below is a diagram illustrating some of the ways in which desertification can be tackled. How many can you identify? Of course, they would not all be found in the same area, but all have been operated successfully in different parts of the world.

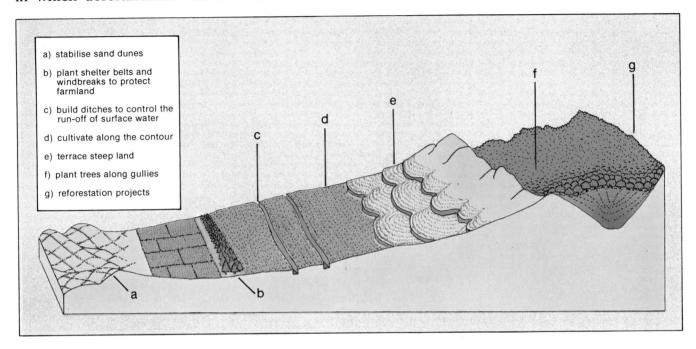

a) stabilise sand dunes

b) plant shelter belts and windbreaks to protect farmland

c) build ditches to control the run-off of surface water

d) cultivate along the contour

e) terrace steep land

f) plant trees along gullies

g) reforestation projects

Working it out

Try this experiment to test whether it is better to cultivate along a slope or down it:

- *Using corrugated plastic, make an artificial 'slope', with the ridges on the plastic running vertically.*
- *Cover the plastic with sand. What happens when water is poured on to the slope?*
- *Now make a slope with the ridges running horizontally. Repeat the experiment.*
What do your results show?

You can also experiment with ways of preventing soil erosion.

- *Start with wet and dry sand. What happens when you blow air from a hairdrier or fan on to the sand?*
- *Devise several types of 'wind break', using different materials and different methods of construction. Which type is most effective?*
N.B. Keep fans/hairdriers away from the water you are using.

The real solution

Above are some of the methods used to combat the spread of deserts. But such methods will not work on their own. The underlying causes of desertification must be tackled.

In the fourth chapter, three main causes of desertification were identified. What were they? It should follow that these should be the main focus for preventing the spread of deserts.

Stopping overcultivation

One way to stop more and more land being used for crop production is to improve what is already there. But any scheme to produce more crops from the same area of land without damaging it must be carefully thought out and involve many different approaches:

- **Improved, drought-resistant varieties** Improved varieties of traditional crops like millet and sorghum could increase yields, although they tend to lose their original drought-resistance and need fertilizers.

- **Fertilizers** Yields of millet and maize can be doubled by applying fertilizers. But fertilizers are expensive and many farmers have to borrow in order to afford them. After a bad year they may find themselves in debt and unable to buy seed for the following year. Artificial fertilizers may themselves damage the soil if used too frequently or incorrectly.

- **Better storage facilities for grain** It is vital to have reserves of grain for drought years when crops fail. Mauritania in north-west Africa has built a national network of grain silos.

- **Better cultivation methods** Higher production can mean that farmers are able to return to traditional methods such as crop rotation, in which a variety of crops are grown in successive years, followed by a fallow period. A common four-year sequence is millet, cowpeas, groundnuts and fallow. Cowpeas provide fodder for cattle and also enrich the soil.

- **Small-scale market gardens and orchards near wells** Villagers' nutrition and food production can be improved by establishing small vegetable and fruit farms in irrigated areas.

- **New crops** Crops like grain amaranth, lima bean, and papago cushaw squash have been shown to be very resistant to drought. A greater variety of crops means that there is less likelihood of a total crop failure.

- **Better irrigation** Good irrigation projects can greatly increase crop production.

Right This crop of grain sorghum grown in North Carolina, USA, is naturally drought-resistant. *Far right* An experimental crop of Lima bean is tested for its suitability for drought conditions.

LIMA BEANS
COMMON NAME
PHASEOLUS LUNATUS
SCIENTIFIC NAME
STRIPPED RED
CULTIVAR

Stopping overgrazing

There are several reasons for overgrazing. Check them again in the fourth chapter. Again, there are no simple answers to the problem. Many of the measures suggested, if used on their own, only cause further problems. They are only successful when used in combination:

- **Improving the quality of animals** Diseases can be controlled through vaccination and other health programmes. As well as being fairer to the animals, this makes economic sense — a sick animal is only a burden to the herders. But higher survival rates lead to bigger herds; bigger herds lead to destruction of grazing land. So better disease control works only if other methods are used too.

- **Better breeds** Most cattle are unsuited to arid and semi-arid conditions; they are not used to travelling long distances in search of water or pasture. Cattle are also susceptible to disease, and cannot withstand drought as effectively as sheep or goats. But they are favoured by herders because of their size and high milk production. Research into

The 'cattle' of the future? The Addax is already well adapted to its North African habitat.

breeds more like those that already inhabit the region, like the addax, a wild (and now threatened) antelope of the Sahara, may produce a more suitable domestic animal.

- **Increasing the number of animals slaughtered** This is not as easy as it sounds. It is important to understand that the herders' animals are not just a form of currency or money; they are part of their life and society. In addition, most of the trade involves the exchange of animals and milk for grain from farmers. When grain itself is scarce, little trade can take place.

- **Improving the range lands** Reducing livestock levels means that the land recovers naturally. Re-seeding projects in the Sudan have also been successful.

- **Better management** Look back at some of the ways in which herders and farmers co-operated in the fourth chapter. Now new systems of management are being attempted. One approach has been to impose grazing controls on nomadic herders, another to encourage them to settle down. In fact, the nomads themselves have always controlled their use of water and pasture. Like the Aboriginal and African bushmen, they understand the land better than anybody. Settlement projects have generally proved fairly disastrous, causing damaging concentrations of animals, as well as harming the way of life of the people themselves.

It would be easy to say that what is needed is a return to the traditional ways, but conditions have changed so much that a return would now be impossible. What is needed is a combination of traditional methods and new techniques, such as better breeding, disease control and better marketing and prices.

Stopping deforestation

'Niger's forests and woodlands will, at the present rate of loss, be exhausted within 20 years'

'About four million hectares of woodland are being cleared each year in the world's drylands. Almost none of it is being replaced.'

'Without the active support and participation of local people, it will be difficult to meet tree planting needs.'

These statements demonstrate both the problems and the answers to the loss of forests. Trees play a vital role in preventing desertification. They can be used in several ways:

- **Combining agriculture and forestry (agroforestry)** Trees are planted in such a way that crop or livestock production can continue. The technique uses 'multi-purpose' trees which can be grown on poor

Burkina Faso. This was a thickly-wooded area before 1970. Few trees now remain.

soil to yield food, fodder (animal feed), fuel wood, building timber and enrich the soil at the same time. One such tree is the acacia. It fertilizes the soil by adding nitrogen and phosphorus; its pods are high in protein and carbohydrate, and crops such as wheat and millet can be grown underneath it.

- **Shelter belts** Trees provide shelter from wind and rain for crops, livestock and soil.

- **Involving people (social forestry)** The most successful afforestation schemes have been those where all members of the community are involved. They are often small projects, based around villages, where the people understand the importance of forests and benefit directly from the work.

Shelter belts

The state of Rajasthan in India is involved in a five-year project to plant 1,500 km of roadside shelterbelts, using trees which can be harvested for fodder and fuel wood.

In north-west China 700,000 farmers established a shelter belt over 1,500 km long and 12 m wide in two seasons.

In the Majia Valley, Niger, a windbreak scheme has increased cereal production by 15 per cent. Now fuel wood can be harvested from the shelter.

Cactus used as a windbreak in Nigeria.

These women will position the brushwood on the sand dunes to cut down the drifting effect of the wind.

Involving the community

Relief agencies work with the local people to protect the land.

This is the single most important lesson to learn in the fight against the spread of deserts. It is only by involving the people who are directly affected that success will be achieved and the spread arrested, perhaps even turned back. Only if they understand the reasons for changing their way of doing things, will the change itself occur. And then only if the action taken is right for that particular area will success eventually be achieved.

The third chapter discussed the sequence of events that takes place when a desert spreads, and the point at which that sequence becomes irreversible. The worse a piece of land is eroded, the more costly it is to reclaim and the longer it takes. But it can be done.

Yet any attempt seems tiny compared with the desert's steady spread. What is needed is for governments to recognize the urgency of the situation, to produce national plans to tackle the problem, and to carry them out. Even more importantly, there is a need for the international community (the nations of the world acting together) to change the conditions that cause deserts. These conditions have little to do with droughts, too many people or bad luck; they are to do with poverty, the balance between cash and food crops and bad land management. Until these are changed, the deserts will go on spreading and people will go on dying.

Above This new forest has been planted in Tunisia in a successful attempt to turn back the spreading desert.

Left Terracing slopes in Ethiopia. Terracing increases the area of land available and slows down the rate at which water runs off the soil.

What can we do to help?

You may not believe it but the spread of deserts affects you, in all sorts of ways. It may well be happening in your own country, so it is costing the nation money, it is damaging your environment, it is possibly even affecting your weather. Even if it is not a particularly big problem where you are, you know that problems do not stop conveniently at national boundaries; they go on echoing round the world.

You may feel that the spread of deserts creates hardship for people in other countries, but that they are not your concern. This is a matter of opinion: whose concern are they? Where do you draw the line? Your family? People you like? People you know?

'There are so many other problems in the world, the spread of deserts is just another one.' If you are thinking along these lines, you are right: there are many other environmental problems – acid rain, pollution, the loss of tropical forests. All of these are major problems but you may be surprised to find that many of the underlying reasons are the same.

Taking action

A famous writer and philosopher, Edmund Burke, said: 'Nobody made a greater mistake than he who did nothing because he could only do a little.' It is easy to do nothing; it can be hard to do a little. Here are a few ideas; no doubt you can think of others.

- **Footpaths and tracks** Try to avoid walking more than two abreast. As paths become wider, they become more susceptible to the effects of wind and rain, and the rate of erosion increases.

- **Look for examples of erosion where you live or go to school** Think how they might be prevented, for example by signs or temporary fences. (This may be possible in the school or youth club grounds;

Soil erosion occurs everywhere. This is in the Peak District, one of Britain's National Parks. What do you think has caused erosion here?

but you need to consult various people first!) How would you encourage people to understand and respect what you are doing? (Think back to what makes afforestation and other projects successful).

- **Join an organization** which helps in the fight against the spread of deserts and other environmental problems, such as the World Wide Fund for Nature (WWF). A list of organizations can be found at the back of this book.

- **Find out to what extent soil erosion is a problem in your own country and how it is being tackled.** There will be a government ministry responsible for the environment and also for agriculture. This might be a good place to start.

- **Join a local nature conservation organization** These organizations campaign to protect areas of countryside and the wildlife dependent on it. Your library should have information about organizations in your area.

- **Keep yourself informed** Read newspapers (which now carry many environmental stories) and magazines, and look out for useful television programmes.

- **Keep others informed** Help them to understand some of the problems and what *they* can do too.

- **Find out more about how our lifestyle affects environments elsewhere** The price we pay for many products that come from cash crops is usually very low. This means the people who work for the cash crop companies earn low wages, or receive a poor price if they grow the crop themselves. We have seen there is a link between poor people and the spread of deserts. Poor people cannot afford to plan or conserve for the future. You may consider it important enough to write to the companies in your own country who use cash crop products, asking for their views. You could write or talk to your local politician. Most aid agencies (Oxfam, for example) produce good advice on how do to this.

The poorer countries of the world are dependent on income from the export of cash crops: tea, coffee, or as here, sugar cane. Yet, by growing cash crops, their land is damaged further.

43

Darkness falls over a parched and broken land and over those who try to eke an existence from it. There is no simple answer to the problem of desertification; but some answers are urgently needed and we all have a part to play in conserving our world.

44

Glossary

Adaptations Ways in which living things have developed, over thousands of years to make the best use of their surroundings.

Afforestation The organized planting of trees, usually to replace those cut down.

Arid Dry lands, usually having an annual rainfall of between 20-25 cm; semi-arid lands have 25-60 cm.

Black market The ways in which goods that are often in short supply are sold illegally, often at very high prices.

Cash crop A crop grown for export (sale abroad) to increase the amount of income from other countries (foreign exchange). Coffee, cotton and tobacco are major cash crops.

Crop rotation The growing of different crops in successive years to prevent exhaustion of the soil. Often the area is left fallow for one of the years.

Deforestation The clearing of forests without replacing them.

Desertification The spread of deserts due to the influence of human beings.

Developing countries Generally applies to countries not using Western (European/American) technology, or apparently not enjoying as high a standard of living. However, such technology may not be appropriate, as the countries may wish to develop in different ways.

Drought resistance A term describing the ability of some crops to withstand low rainfall and periods of drought.

Erosion The loss of soil, usually by the action of wind or rain.

Evaporation The loss of water into the atmosphere as water vapour.

Fallow A method of farming in which cultivated land is allowed to lie 'idle' for one or more years, to allow it to recover.

Grazing controls Attempts to restrict the movement of nomadic herders in order to prevent erosion.

Gullies Channels, usually worn by rain running rapidly off land. They increase the rate of erosion and make the land more difficult to cultivate.

Humidity The amount of moisture (water vapour) contained in the atmosphere.

Humus Dead plant or animal matter in the soil; a high humus content allows the soil to retain large amounts of water, and improves its structure.

Intensive farming Methods, such as the use of fertilizers or machinery, that allow more crops or livestock to be raised on a particular area of land.

Irrigation Methods, such as building canals or digging wells, that bring water to dry areas.

Migration The regular movement of people or animals, often over large distances, to obtain better living conditions.

Nomads People who do not settle in one place, but continually move across a country, taking all their possessions, including their livestock, with them.

Nutrients Substances in the soil, such as nitrates and phosphates, which help plant growth.

Resource Anything that can be used by living things. Examples include land, water and minerals.

Sahel Countries on the edge of the Sahara.

Salinization The process by which water, usually from irrigation projects, becomes increasingly salty until crops can no longer grow.

United Nations The assembly where most of the world's countries are represented. It attempts to deal with international problems.

Warm-blooded Animals (mammals and birds) that are able to keep their body temperature constant despite changes in the surrounding temperature. Cold-blooded animals (reptiles, amphibians, insects etc.) are unable to do this, although they may have some control over their body temperature.

Water table The level at which water is permanently present under the soil (ground water).

Yield The amount of a crop or other product that is harvested or otherwise obtained.

Further reading

An Atlas of World Wildlife Sir Julian Huxley (ed.) (Mitchell Beazley, 1974)
Cultivating Hunger: an Oxfam study of food, power and poverty (Oxfam, 1985)
Desertification: how people make deserts, how people can stop and why they don't Alan Grainger (Earthscan, 1982)
Deserts K. Lye (Wayland, 1987)
The Facts of Life: vital information for all concerned with World Hunger (Oxfam information pack, 1984)

The Future for the Environment Mark Lambert (Wayland, 1986)
Harvest of Dust (audiovisual, UNEP, 1985)
Hot Deserts Roger Clare (Edward Arnold, 1978)
The Living Planet David Attenborough (BBC, 1984)
'Only One Earth' Education Pack (WWF United Kingdom/North South Productions/International Institute for Environment and Development, 1987)

Useful addresses

Alice Springs Conservation
  Organization
PO Box 2796
Alice Springs
N.T. 5750

Australian Association for
  Environmental Education
GPO Box 112
Canberra
ACT 2601

Council for Environmental
  Education
School of Education
University of Reading
London Road
Reading RG1 5AQ

Friends of the Earth (Australia)
National Liaison Office
366 Smith Street
Collingwood
Victoria 3065

Friends of the Earth (Canada)
Suite 53
54 Queen Street
Ottawa KP5 C5

Friends of the Earth (New
  Zealand)
Nagal House
Courthouse Lane
PO Box 39/065
Auckland West

Friends of the Earth (UK)
26−28 Underwood Street
London N1 7JC

Friends of the Earth (USA)
530 7th Street SE
Washington DC 20003

International Centre for
  Conservation Education
Greenfield House
Guiting Power
Cheltenham
Gloucester G154

Oxfam
274 Banbury Road
Oxford OX2 7DZ

UNEP (United Nations
  Environment Programme)
PO Box 30552
Nairobi
Kenya

WATCH
22 The Green
Nettleham
Lincolnshire

World Wide Fund for Nature UK
  (WWF)
Panda House
Weyside Park
Godalming
Surrey GU7 1QU

Index

Picture acknowledgements

The photographs in this book were supplied by: Bruce Coleman Ltd, by the following photographers: Paul Wakefield 4; B. & C. Calhoun 5 (top); J. Cancalosi 5 (bottom right); John R. Brownlie 8; Jen & Des Bartlett 11 (bottom right); Sullivan & Rogers 12; Steve Kaufman 13; Henneghien 16; Ken Lambert 17; L. C. Marigo 18 (left); B. & C. Alexander 24; Peter Davey 28; David Austen 29; Erwin & Peggy Bauer 37; Hutchison Library 6, 7, 23, 25, 30, 36 (right), 41 (bottom); Frank Lane Picture Agency 11 (top, bottom left), 18 (right), 42; Peter Newark's Western Americana 19; Christine Osborne Pictures 20, 26, 32, 41 (top); Oxfam Picture Library, by the following photographers: Jeremy Hartley 21, 23, 33, 38, 39, 40; Nick Haslam 31; Anna Tulley 39; F. Rubin 43; Oxford Scientific Films, by the following photographers: Rodger Jackman 5 (bottom right); David Curl 14; Jack Dermid 36 (centre); ZEFA Picture Library 44 and by the following photographers: Robin Smith 15; Foto Leidman cover. All artwork is by Marilyn Clay.